C000271488

GARDEN OF ASHES

GARDEN OF ASHES

Cookie Mueller

HANUMAN EDITIONS

This volume first published by Hanuman
Books in 1990.

© 1990, 2023, Max Mueller

Cover photo © Bobby Miller

ISBN 979-8-9893780-3-6

Printed in the UK.
Typeset in Arnhem Fine, with Eksell and
Caslon No540 Swash D.

Hanuman Editions
London & Seattle
hanumaneditions.com

Contents

Cookie Mueller

COOKIE MUELLER

Born 1949 Baltimore, Maryland

Biography and Education: I received most of my education traveling and working various inane jobs such as: clothing designer, racehorse hot walker, drug dealer, go-go dancer, underground film actress (otherwise known as independent feature actress), theater actress, playwright, theater director, performance artist, house cleaner, fish packer, credit clerk, barmaid, sailor, high seas cook, film script doctor, herbal therapist, unwed welfare mother, film extra, leg model, watercolorist, and briefly as a bar mitzvah entertainer, although I'm not even Jewish.

I started writing when I was six and have never stopped completely. I wrote a novel when I was twelve and put it in cardboard and Saran Wrap, took it to the library and put it on the shelves in the correct alphabetical order. When I was eighteen I left college for Haight-Ashbury and wound up a drug casualty, not unlike a bag lady. I learned a lot in the mental hospital, where I had shock therapy chat didn't work except for eradicating from my memory all the contents from novels I had read in the past twelve years.

A few of the films I appeared in have attained a cult status and I am told that I have a fan club in Los Angeles.

I have a twelve-year-old son, who I believe has taught me the most.

I used to write poetry, but now I feel that poetry is archaic unless written specifically as song lyrics. I believe that my short stories are novels for people with short attention spans. I live with my son in Manhattan and pay the rent as a journalist.

Alien

ALIEN—1965

I was always leaving. Every time I left
I had a different hair color and I would
be standing on the porch saying good-
bye to the older couple in the living
room. I didn't have anything in com-
mon with them except that we shared
a few inherited chromosomes, the
identical last name, and the same
bathroom.

They would be protesting. Scream-
ing. It became a tune, with the same
refrain, and the same lyrics, "If you

leave now, you'll have no future. If you leave now, you'll be a bum."

"I'll be back in the fall when school starts." Or "I'll be back after the weekend."

"If you leave now, don't dare come back. How are you going to live? You don't have any money. Why do you have to leave?"

"It's natural. It's a biological urge. Like little birds testing their wings. I can't help myself."

There were a bunch of people waiting for me, in the street in front of the house, honking the horn of a cream

T-bird, or a black Impala convertible,
or a pale blue Rambler.

"Bye, I'll see you soon."

"Do you want some money?"

"No. Thanks anyway. Bye."

We sped off. I told my friends in
the car that I was an alien to my parents. It was better that I didn't hang
around there too much. At this point
it would always dawn on me that there
was another problem. Not only was I
alien to my parents, but I was an alien
to my friends.

Breaking Into
Show Bizz

BREAKING INTO SHOW BIZZ
Baltimore, 1969

I was living in a little cavelike hideaway on an alley called Lovegrove. The only door of this dugout lair opened directly on the alley, so that made it seem like secret chambers. It was odd. It had character.

This place must have had a seedy history, because it was alive with uneasy spirits. Maybe, in former days, it had been an all-night opium den, or

the clandestine hutch for felons who
have their pictures in the post office.
It was definitely an undercover joint.
Perhaps it was a speakeasy during pro-
hibition, or a cubbyhole for occultists,
even a bomb shelter. Ir just wasn't a
normal living space, by any standards.

I still have nightmares about this
place.

It had two rooms plus the kitchen
and bathroom, which were always dark
because the three meager windows that
looked out on the alley never saw sunlight, just dense eternal twilight. I kept
them draped with heavy velvet. Its low

ceilings were covered with a jumble of exposed pipes.

Living there I felt like a mole.

The only way I could make the place livable was to layer it with dark fabrics and light it with tons of candles. All the heavy curtains and yard goods muffled city sounds. I could have been anywhere. The silence and the candle-light made reality impossible. It began to look cozy like a medieval padded cell for alchemist wizards.

I lived there with my pet monkey who liked cockroaches. He used to scan the fabric walls for them. When he saw

one from all the way across the room
with his primate super X-ray vision, he'd
swing the distance on the ceiling pipes
and deftly scoop up the bug with one
hand, pop it in his mouth, and swing
back to the curtain rod window perch
where he lived. He was a good pet.

There were always a few people
living there with me, they floated in
and out, but a pretty lesbian named
Babette, who never wore a shirt in-
doors, and a homeless philosopher
hippie named Nash were permanent
fixtures on the sofa. We lived primarily
on LSD, poppy seed buns, and cheap

champagne. Nash sold LSD from the place, so this paid the rent.

I was working on some novel, long since lost in the shuffle, and the word "future" wasn't part of my vocabulary. This was my status when I accidentally broke into show biz.

At the time in Baltimore, there'd been word of a hometown filmmaker named John Waters who was showing his low-budget films in churches and bingo halls all over the city. One night, Babette, Nash and I went to one of his screenings of *Mondo Trasho* at a church bingo hall, right around the corner from Lovegrove Alley.

A door prize was offered and after the screening there was a random drawing of ticket stubs. I won.

The prize was twofold: dinner at a White Tower Hamburger joint and a screen test. Over dinner I discovered John Waters and he discovered me. We got along.

John was as thin as a string bean with shoulder-length brown hair and a pencil-thin mustache. He wore thrift-store shirts, drank Coca-Cola, and smoked Kool Midgets nonstop. He made me laugh.

He seemed driven, so driven in fact, that when he told me that he was pre-mature and only weighed a pound at birth, I envisioned him as an infant, compact like a pound cake, lying in a clear plastic preemie life support box, while nurse's aides were off loafing, al-ready rococo and bursting his bunting wrapper with his dreams and plans of film scenarios. I'm sure he was enter-taining the other babies, making them laugh about the inept hospital staff, their moms and dads, and the oddness of being born. He's one of those kinds of people that you imagine was already an adult while still a baby. The same, just smaller.

When later I did the screen rest and met the bunch of actors who were his constant companions, Divine, Mink Stole, David Lockhary, Bonnie Pierce, Pat Moran, Susan Lowe, Marina Melin, I felt like I was meeting my new family. I got a part in his next film, *Multiple Maniacs*. We were starting to shoot in a couple of weeks.

I'd found a new niche, a foray as an underground film actress. So there I was, way way underground, figuratively and literally, underground in the

Lovegrove inner sanctum studying the underground script by candlelight.

Being underground times two felt right.

I came above ground when the alley home flooded during a four-day rainstorm and Babette and Nash left for a Russian River, California, commune. I moved to an attic apartment with lots of sunlight.

*Waiting for
the New Age*

WAITING FOR
THE NEW AGE

One day in the park, a helicopter
swooped in and dropped little pills
of LSD on everybody. They said it
was Owsley himself up there, but
who knew for sure? We ate them.
Didn't matter who sent them to us.

That day we were certain everything was finally going to happen like
we'd been hoping.

The San Andreas fault and the old
fault over there under New York City

were going to act up, rumble, crack, and destroy California and the East Coast, Colorado would have beach-front property.

There'd only be a few places on the earth that wouldn't sink into the depths. Those would be the Power Places that existed on earth's meridians where life force energy accumulated. Places like where the Great Pyramid of Giza or Stonehenge stood, or the Nazca plains where UFOs have their airstrip, Machu Picchu, Mount Everest, Lake Titicaca, the Bermuda Triangle, Easter Island, and of course, Golden

Gate Park in San Francisco.

Mostly everything would be destroyed, all the corporation buildings, banks, and industrial plants anyway, but communes, ashrams, retreats, and hippies' homes and gardens would stand. People who weren't wise or spiritual enough would fall into the cracks and go the way of the dinosaurs. It'd be the end for people of their kind.

Atlantis and Mu would of course rise again from the oceans and the new generation, the sons and daughters of the Light, the lost tribe, the descendants and reincarnates of

Atlantis and Mu would inherit the earth, which of course would suddenly bounce back and abound with lush green, wonderful flora and fauna, and clean sparkling air and water.

We'd dance around in peace, love, sunshine, flowers. We'd swim with the dolphins and whales to share insights. Yes, we'd be the ones saved to start the new world. Things would be great. There'd be no wars, hatred, fear, or insensitivity... all living things would communicate telepathically, including our brothers and sisters, the plants.

There'd be plenty of other great

stuff. Everybody would be able to
see each other's auras as halo lights
around their heads. White and blue
auras would be the most spiritual
colors. The healers would have green
lights. Yellow lights for those in-
between types. Some people would
have red auras, which isn't so great
but might be okay if they controlled
their wild tempers.

Everything was all predestined and
arranged and we knew these things
without really having to discuss them.

We waited all day for the first rumble of the big quake, and the first crash

of thunder, and force of wind that would beckon in the earth's rebirth. But it didn't happen that day. We didn't lose hope though. We waited until the next day and then the next three days. Then time stretched out and we waited through all the days in Haight-Ashbury.

Knowing that we were the blessed ones in states of grace, we lived clean lives in preparedness and took drugs to kill time. We got ready with our backpacks and energy granola.

We practiced astrology, yoga, levitation, transcendental meditation, astral travel, telekinesis, cabalism, prayer. We called on the spirits. We waited and waited, and hoped, but the world didn't fall apart. It was a big letdown.

Finally low-level energy swept through the Haight, destroying plans for the coming age. Some people gave up and became computer programmers or realtors.

But some people are still waiting, right there on Hippie Hill. Waiting and hoping. Still watching for the end.

"Look around," they say, "Mark our words. It won't be with a bang."

Edith Massey:
A Star

EDITH MASSEY: A STAR

On location for *Multiple Maniacs* in Baltimore's Fell's Point, after a long day of shooting, we'd all go over to Pete's Hotel Bar for a fifteen-cent draft beer, or a fifty-cent mixed drink. Pete's was a flophouse bar where Edith Massey was a barmaid. We'd all talk show biz there.

Pete's had fluorescent lights, peeling paint, and loose linoleum on the floor. It was a generic bar, just stools, a couple of tables, some mirrors, and a wooden bar that ran the length of the place.

The clientele of Pete's were old barflies, all of them down and our alcoholics, former stevedores, retired factory workers, ex-B-girls, and waitresses too tired and old to wait anymore. The years of booze had taken their toll on these people's looks, their faces were wrinkled and puffy, with bulbous rugged noses covered in gin blossoms (broken blood vessels) like pink golf balls with thin red spiders on them.

The liquor hadn't dampened their spirits though, they were always laugh-

ing in their beer. All of them lived in
the neighborhood, Fell's Point. It was
the low-rent district. The only ocher
types aside from bums and boozers
who lived around there were a
smattering of poor visionary artists.

It was the oldest section of Baltimore, really just a bunch of little two-
story houses built in the early 1800s.
At the time, 1969, the streets were still
cobblestoned, there were lots of quiet
little bars, corner dime variety stores,
family-run grocery stores. This part of
town was not unlike the worse part of
the Bowery, but unlike the Bowery it

was pretty, it had lots of charm. It was the old harbor section, it sat right on the deserted, dilapidated docks with the expansive sky awash with light reflected off the water. This was the kind of place, this quaint enclave of the city, that would later be discovered by the developers and the yuppies who would buy the houses, renovate them into early Americana, sell them, or live in them.

But then there were lots of flophouses, soup kitchens, and bars, in fact, five bars to every block. My friends who lived there had houses for sixty dollars a month. Vince Peranio, the artist who created all John's film sets, had a huge three-storied former warehouse/bakery for a hundred a month.

Vince was the one who first started going to Pete's Bar, who met Edith, and like everyone else, loved his bartender. Vince introduced Edith to John there. He saw star quality in her; she was the real thing.

John cast her in *Multiple Maniacs* as Jesus's mother. She was thrilled, she had always wanted to be a star, in fact when she was sixteen, she ran away to Hollywood to become a star. She got as far in the film biz as working in a street booth selling pencils and combs and razor blades to aspiring actors and actresses. As she saw it, these were the implements of the trade: a pencil to write down the casting agent's address, a comb to fix your hair for the film audition, and a razor blade to cut your wrists when you didn't get the part.

Edith did get into show biz, on stage as a dancer in strip joints. She danced her way across the country, hitchhiking, hopping freight trains. She once owned her own bar in Calumet City, Illinois, and she was a madam in a place in Talihina, Oklahoma, that used a hotdog stand as a front.

She was one of the sweetest women, she fed the stray cats, she brought American cheese and Wonderbread sandwiches to the bums on the street. She could barely afford to do this. She wore her long dark hair in a forties' poof in the front, the back hung down almost to her waist; she wore the same dresses she'd worn in the forties. She had warts on her nose, there was a large space between her front teeth, she hardly ever drank, but when she did she was funny, she had a thick

Baltimore accent, and she was everyone's mother confessor.

With her part in *Multiple Maniacs*, she was finally in films. She wasn't a quick study, though. When she memorized her part, she would memorize her screen directions too and say them right along with her lines during shooting. John had to do a million takes, but she was worth it; she was such a great terrible actress, the best.

When *Multiple Maniacs* opened she thought her life would change, she thought Hollywood agents would call her at Pete's Hotel Bar. They didn't.

In the years to come, she was the Egg Lady in *Pink Flamingos*, Aunt Ida in *Female Trouble*, the reigning queen in *Desperate Living*. In between films she opened a junk shop, Edith Shopping Bag in Fell's Point, where autograph hounds would come to be near her, and listen to her rambling chatter, while she sat at the cash register in her house dress and her skuffies. With her kitties and her fans all around her, she was happy.

I used to stop in there every day, since my thirty-dollar-a-month apartment was right around the corner.

Sometimes in the junk shop I'd see something I liked.

One day I took off my jacket to try on a coat hanging on a rack and by the time I was finished, Edith had accidentally sold my own jacket to a shopper.

"Aw, hon, I'm seow sarry. I'll geev ya the moneee, I gaot fave dallers foor it," she was very apologetic, "I dint neew what ta cheearg foor it, dere weernt neo teag oon it or nuthin. I'm sarry, hon. Yeoo woont aunther ceoat, yeoo teak it, hon. Leok reound, deres seam perrty ceoats heer."

It had been my favorite jacket, but

one could never get mad at Edith.

"It's okay, hon," I said, "Maybe I can still catch the person who bought it." I looked up and down the street but the happy shopper was gone.

"Heer, yeoo teak the fave dallers," she handed me the bill.

"No, Edith," I said, "I'll just put on the coat I was tryin on. It's nice. I like it."

Years later Edith actually moved to Hollywood and opened a junk shop there. She was finally a star in Hollywood.

Once when she was visiting me in

New York on business, singing in her nightclub review, we went out at seven A.M. to Washington Square Park to feed the pigeons. She bought nuts and popcorn especially for them.

"Ain't they cute?" she asked while the fat pigeons fluttered in around her. Sitting on the park bench, in the morning sun, amid the sanitation workers dumping the overflowing mesh garbage cans, and elderly people moving by with their aluminum walkers, she started her usual stream-of-consciousness chatter. She talked about her new stray kitty that was once a street rat catcher, who was so mangy and hair-less she put an infant's blue sweater on him until he could grow some more fur. They were all kitties to her.

She went silent after that. Then she said something I haven't forgotten. Perhaps she was suddenly taking stock of her life.

"John Werters is ah wunerfeol mean," she told me, "Heez been sea neez ta mee. Hee mead mee a stoar, Cookie. I'd prally stal bea barmead witheealt heam. Hee mead mee a stoar."

"You were always a star Edith. You

would have been a star without John.
He just made you a FAMOUS star," I
told her.

She was a star indeed.

Tattooed Friends

TATTOOED FRIENDS

Susan unscrewed a bottle of rotgut port, the kind laced with formaldehyde, and sat down at the kitchen table where black mollies swam in a blown glass oval and a potted hibiscus was folding up its red blossoms for the night. Mardi Gras beads at the window moved and clicked in the first timid breeze of the twilight. It was as if the rising moon had exhaled a cool sigh.

The sun sank on the wood plank terrace right out the window, where

Susan had left her unfinished canvas and open tubes of paint.

"Oughtta cap up those tubes, Sue," I said.

"They'll be okay," she said. "It's not gonna rain tonight."

"I'll do it," I went out the window and put the caps I could find on the tubes. The sky was getting dark royal blue and there was the moon like a white banana. Next to it was Venus, the first star to appear at twilight and the last one to fade at dawn, as large as a glowing ping-pong ball.

"This would make a good tattoo,"

I called to Susan and she looked up
from the table at the configuration of
Venus and the crescent moon. We'd
been talking about tattoos earlier, in
the heat of the day.

"Too Turkish," she said.

"Yeah, you're right. It looks just like
their flag." I went back into the window.

"Why don't we give ourselves some
tattoos? Right now." She was all excited,
"I have all the stuff to do it."

"I guess it's time to have a tattoo," I
nodded. It was inevitable. I was following in my grandfather's footsteps. He
was a sailor and a tugboat captain, with

lots of girls and anchors on his arms. My mother hated them, the same way she would hate mine.

"What though?" I asked Sue. While I pondered, I started drawing little experimental designs on pieces of paper. "It has to be something I won't get tired of since I'm going to have it for the rest of my life."

"How about this?" she pointed to the spot right below her left elbow on the topside where she'd just penned her Capricorn astrological sign on her skin.

"Good idea," I said. "Why don't you

put your Pisces sign in the same place?" she suggested.

"Great!" I said. "Let's do it."

This was perfect. We wouldn't get tired of these little tattoos. She would always be a Capricorn, I'd always be a Pisces. That wouldn't ever change. It wouldn't be like tattooing the name of your current boyfriend.

I drew a quarter-inch Pisces symbol in the same place on my own arm where Susan had drawn hers. It looked good.

Susan brought in some sewing needles, white cotton thread, a candle, and India ink. We wrapped the sewing needles with the thread, sterilized them in the candle flame, dipped them into the India ink and started punching our flesh with the needle points, following the outline of the penned-in symbols on the skin.

"I knew this one guy who tattooed himself in jail with the point of a guitar string," she said, "I guess they didn't have any sewing needles."

"Why is it only people in jail do tattoos?" I wondered.

"I guess they're bored," she said.

"Or maybe they just don't have any paper to draw on, " I said.

These were our first tattoos. We needed tattoos. We didn't know why. It was something bigger than both of us. Maybe we'd both been North African Berber women in past lives.

After this first tattoo, I was hooked. Through the years, I couldn't stop tattooing myself. I thought of it as body decoration. I never wanted to be too nude, even without clothes. Now, I'd always be a little dressed.

Six tattoos and four years after the first one, I used to go to this nude beach called Ballston Beach in North Truro, Massachusetts, on Cape Cod.

This nude beach scene was a one-summer phenomenon. It was a mini Isle of Levant, quite a show, before the tourists came to gawk and the police started jailing people for indecent exposure.

On beach blankets bare butts were broiling in the sun like luscious ham hocks. Pubic hair unfurled in the breeze. Nude people played volleyball with their dingdongs dangling and boobs bouncing in tune with the game scores.

Everyone was naked as jaybirds and my tattoos were turning heads. Nudies were wearing hats, and some of them sneakers, but no one was wearing a tattoo, except for this old nude Wellfleet oyster fisherman, who was always doing pencil sketches of the girls frolicking in the surf.

This was before it became sort of fashionable for women to have tattoos. The untattooed masses saw my Pisces sign on my arm, the moon on my shoulder, the falcon on my wrist, the dots on my fingers, and an eternity symbol, a lizard eating its tail, on my leg. Strangers started approaching me.

"I love your tattoos," they'd stare.

"What's this one on your thigh? What do the ones on your hands mean? Are these occult symbols? Did it hurt? Who did them?" When I told them I did them myself, they all wanted me to tattoo them. I started bringing the India ink and needles to the beach with me. Every day under the sun, I tattooed people who were committed to a life of wearing insignia.

"This isn't a decision to be taken lightly," I told them, "You're gonna have this for the rest of your life, so you better think about it."

To the people that asked me, "So

what do you think I should have?" I
told them to go home and think about
it for a week. To the people that came
around and said, "Right here I want a
pyramid and an eyeball," and they had
already penned it on the skin spot, I
got out the sanitary needles and was
ready to punch it in.

Everybody wanted tattoos that
summer. I worked on shoulders,
ankles, backs, breasts. Thighs, asses,
and foreheads. I tried to talk people
out of having tattoos of Mickey Mouse
or Huey, Dewey, and Louie ducks, or
their girlfriends' names. People on

LSD or mushrooms wanted stars or third eyes in the middle of their fore-heads, but I told them to come back when they felt a little more grounded, less far-out.

"You might regret it someday," I'd say. "Suppose you wanted to become a film actor someday. How many movie roles do you think people with face tattoos might get? Put the third eye on your ass instead."

A lot of people got tattoos that summer. Some got hooked.

That following winter, in Province-town, tattoo fever overtook the town.

Everyone was tattooing themselves. The Provincetown art supply store ran out of India ink. There was a run on sewing needles at the five and dime, needle prices went sky high.

All over town, around the candlelit tables, over bottles of ink and pain-killing 151-proof rum, sewing needles were scabbing designs on skin. The liquor store ran our of 151 rum, but we didn't stop, we moved on to tequila.

Cape Cod winters can be brutal and boring or lonely, but not this one. We got to know each other. Tattooing stirred conversation.

It was better than hanging in a bar, more sociable than Canasta, more exciting than Monopoly, as challenging as Scrabble, and cheaper than gambling at poker.

In the old traditional New England way, it was an arty masochist's version of a sewing bee.

Female Trouble

FEMALE TROUBLE

There are some hairdos that make
women look like they've just had a
facelift. Very tight ponytails can do
this, and tight pigtails too. But white
women past twelve years of age look
dumb in pigtails. I did.

The last time I wore them, I didn't
have a choice.

"Your hair was all matted up and
snapping off, you were thrashing
around so much," the hairdo nurse
said.

"I had a pretty high fever?" I asked her.

"Yeah, you were delirious, but you were funny," she laughed.

I'd just woken up in a hospital bed, I didn't know where, but it didn't matter, I felt great, clean, and very neat. My hair was parted down the middle with two tight braids ending in white surgical rubber bands.

John Waters and Mink Stole laughed at me when they saw me with this hairdo in the hospital bed.

"So it didn't turn out to be appendicitis, so what is it? What's wrong with you?" John asked and got comfortable on the foot of the bed.

"Female trouble," I said. It was a catch-all phrase and he found this term very funny... so funny, in fact, it became the tide for his next movie.

"What kind of female trouble?" Mink asked woman to woman.

"Infected Fallopian tubes... PID, you know, nothing too serious," I said. I didn't want to be in the hospital. I was missing the best part of the summer on Cape Cod, but I'd collapsed three days before in a cold sweat before the noon lunch whistle at the

Provincetown Fish Factory where I had a job packing rock lobster tails and freshly caught mackerel. I didn't hate the job, I didn't even hate the smell of fish, or my black rubber apron, gloves, and swash buckling boots that were caked with fish scales. I liked working with the tough townies, the "Portagees," the men and women who were descended from the Portuguese whaling people that settled on the Cape in the early 1800s. I liked their lingo. I got all the town gossip, the inside dirt the tourists never heard.

I guess this illness was going to end

my fish career. From what the doctors
told me, I was going to be in the
hospital for at least two weeks.

"How did you let it go so long?
Weren't you in pain?" Mink asked.

"Yeah, but I thought it was period
cramps or something," I said. Actually
I'd been in lots of pain and I was
worried but I'd been raised to ignore
pain like a strong pioneer woman with
the good genes of the North Carolina
Sawyers. If my mother's Sawyer theory
for illness didn't work, then my Ger-
man father's Mueller theory did...
a couple of tankards of husky beer

always brought the cure.

"We were really worried when we saw you being taken away in an ambulance from Doctor Herbert's, " John said, "Do you remember that?"

"I was kinda out of it," I said, "What'd I look like?"

"Your makeup was fine," Mink assured me.

"Ah... good ole Dr. Herbert," I smiled. He was Provincetown's miracle worker, a rosy-cheeked jolly octogenarian M.D. who didn't believe in pain either. He went down into the annals of medical history as the only doctor who performed an appendectomy on himself. With mirrors. I must have been pretty bad off for him to send me away in an ambulance.

"Good thing the fish factory people brought you to him instead of Dr. Silva," Mink said. There were only two doctors in Provincetown at the time. Doctor Silva was the town's joke doctor. In his waiting room he had framed pictures of Robert Young as Marcus Welby, M.D., and Raymond Jaffe as Doctor Zorba. Vince Edwards as Doctor Casey, with his surgeon's Nehru collar agape wasn't there, and neither was Richard

Chamberlain as Dr. Kildare.

"So when are you getting out?" John asked.

"Dunno," I said.

Eighteen days, and many injections of antibiotics later, my doctor came in to sign me out.

"You're fine now," he said, "The infection is gone, but I've got some bad news."

"Yeah?" I asked. It couldn't be so bad. I was going home.

"It looks like you'll be incapable of conceiving children," he said and after I didn't respond he said, "Of course

I'm not really sure."

He left and while I was discarding my butt-revealing hospital gown and getting into my black Levi's and high-heeled mules, two ocher staff gyne-cologists came in and told me the same news. They looked really sad.

"Hey. It's okay, who wants kids any-way? We're already too many on the earth," I said. But when I envisioned my future, there was a child of my own in it. I guess I'd have to adopt.

Two years later I was back in the same hospital. but this time I was in the maternity ward.

Divine

DIVINE

There is a little hill right outside Provincetown where everything opens up big and wide, the sky, the bay, the sea, and the dunes. From this point you can see the end of the world, or at least the end of America, the very last tip of the Cape jutting into the Atlantic. It's called the Witch's Knoll because supposedly it's where the old broom riders met to toil and trouble over their bubbling brew on full moon coven nights. It's the windiest part of the Cape and the wildest.

From this vantage point on clear winter days, you can see whales blowing their spouts and flicking their tails among huge icebergs from Arctic flows.

The Cape highway runs right over this knoll.

The day Divine and I were traveling along this very spot the wind was kicking and howling, shaking and whipping the VW bus with a lot of force. There was some ice and snow on the road and we didn't have snow tires, but we were singing "Got no diamonds. Got no pearls. Still I think I'm a lucky

girl..." from *Annie Get Your Gun*, and
the day so clear and fresh that we didn't
care about slipping and fishtailing.
We were zooming toward a thrift-store
shopping spree down-Cape.

A mean hand of the wind caught us
while we were on the second verse.
"Got no checkbooks. Got no bank..."
and the bus just spun all the way
around twice and then it just fell over
onto the tall dune grass and almost into
the wild cranberry bog. It just tipped
over like an empty cardboard box.

A funny thing happens in all car
accidents. Time changes. Everything

goes into exaggerated slow motion. It's so bizarre.

Once I was in a really bad car accident with my parents when I was fourteen and while the car was spinning slow and mom and dad were flying out the doors in quarter rime, I was marveling at the eerie time phenomenon. It was only when the car came to a full stop that time sped up again and got normal. The same thing happened this day except neither of us got hurt.

When the VW bus came to a halt on its side and time got regular again, Divine and I found ourselves in the

back of the bus. I was on top of Divine.
The windows were flush to the ground,
and we were dazed, but nothing was
broken. The engine was still whirring
away.

"You alright, Cookie?" he asked me.

"Yeah. You?"

"Yeah. But that was weird. Like slow
motion," he said and crawled into the
front and pushed open the passenger
door that was now the top of the bus.
"Door works." He laughed.

"The windows didn't even break,"
I said looking around and crawling out
after him.

We walked around the bus and stared at its belly. It looked fine. Nothing was falling off.

It wasn't even scratched.

"We gotta call a tow truck or something." I said but a phone was miles away and there weren't any cars coming along.

Divine didn't say a word. He just picked up the bus, the whole thing and stood it up, back on its tires. Just like Superman-woman.

I think I was just standing there with my mouth open.

"God, you're really strong," I said,

"I can't believe you just lifted this thing. I'm flabbergasted. You oughtta go into wrestling or weightlifting or something." I couldn't get over it.

"Must have been adrenaline strength," he said and he got back in the driver's seat. "Well, get in," he said. "We going shopping or what?"

From that day on I always felt really safe when I was with Divine. He wasn't afraid of anything.

Fleeting Happiness

FLEETING HAPPINESS

Many years and brain cells ago, I had this belief that everyone would be happy someday. I have since found that this isn't necessarily so.

Happiness is a fictitious feeling. It was created by imaginative storytellers for the purpose of plot building or story resolution. Fortunately most people don't know this. They think the lives they are living are actual screen-plays or theater pieces. In earlier times people were convinced their lives were the fantastic tales told at the fireside. Because of this, I have seen people stop in their tracks for a moment and wonder where the plot is, but mostly they just forge on blindly.

Believing that life will someday be wonderful isn't a bad thing, in fact it is absolutely necessary. To know the truth—life is hard, and then you die—isn't a very comfortable thing to live with. If everyone knew the cold facts, the sky would be darkened with falling bodies in suicide leaps.

Most people have been led to believe that their lives would be better if they

had money, and usually this isn't
wrong. They know it's not impossible
to come into money, in fact I've read
that every thirty-nine minutes a new
millionaire emerges in the world.

But what's the real reason people
want lots of money? Food? Clothing?
Shelter? Yes, these things are basic,
even the poor often have these things
in modest amounts. Usually, the more
you have of each of these basics, the
more complicated life gets. Having too
much food makes you fat; you need to
diet. Having too many clothes makes it
hard to make a decision in the morning;

you need to organize. Having too many homes must be really tough; you have to fill them. And why own all these things anyway, if there's no one else to share them with, or no one to hire to help you, or no one to be jealous of you?

I have pondered this and come up with the logical answer. People want money because they want to be loved. They believe that money will buy them love. Okay, we've all heard this.

Now, suppose you had lots of money, thus you had tons of lovers (perhaps it's superficial love but this blossoms), and you had lots of servants who loved you and hung around, and you had lots of friends who were envious. You would expect that everything would be great. Lots of love, lots of money. What else could one want?

Unfortunately, the pitiable human being will still want something else. It is human nature.

The next thing to want would be fame. So you need publicity. That's not difficult; you can buy a newspaper or magazine company and put your own name and picture in the headlines if you want; you can finance films and star yourself. Okay, now you have money, love, and fame. But still people laugh at you behind your back. Then what? The answer is power.

Let's suppose your magazine is successful and your film is a box-office smash. Then you have all four: money, love, fame, and power. Would you be happy? No. You would probably go mad.

Look at Howard Hughes. He had all four. In the end he went insane. He was so afraid of germs he was walking around with sanitary Kleenex boxes on his feet.

No one is ever satisfied.

Some people might remind you that the holy men of the East are satisfied, but I don't think so. Even those guys want something. They might want infinite wisdom or they might want to perform miracles to impress followers, or they might want to levitate. It's always something.

Being a human being isn't easy, what with all these insatiable physical, emotional, and intellectual desires.

If the ultimate goal in life is to be happy, then you have to admit that one-celled creatures have it all over us.

Little germs are probably always happy. They are superior, they don't sing the blues. Think about that the next time you bring out the disinfectant bottle and start scrubbing them away.

Look at Howard Hughes again. He must have known that the happiness of germs was something terrifyingly enviable. He must have been jealous.

The Homeless

THE HOMELESS

Drop the leashes on your dogma,
relax the wagging tongue, don't let
your asymmetrical opinions or your
biased hypotheses slither into this
illumination. Offered here will be
a novel way to look at the ancient
manner of living, lately called home-
lessness. These days it's deemed a
pitiable problem, but there was a
time when hardy outdoors people
were revered for their pioneer spirit.
Could it be that some human beings

(providing they are sane) make the conscious choice to live under the stars? Could it be that some people like fresh air twenty-four hours a day?

Instead of thinking of homeless people as human flotsam or scum on the gene pool, we should look at them as superior beings, humans who have painstakingly solved the complex riddle of global existence and are a necessary link in the chain of planetary life. We have to honor them, praise them for their diligent hard work. Forget about seeing them as indigents, welfare beneficiaries, lazy bums; these people are performing a valuable- priceless-service to all human-kind. Did you realize that they're the only honest ecologists alive today? These people are our real recyclers; they eat the food we throw away, they wear the clothes we discard, they live in the boxes we empty. On the famous Goodness and Earth-Awareness Scale these people rate higher... much higher than consumer/users like you. The future of humanity rests in the hands of the bag people and the homeless, not upwardly mobile users.

The lowest human on this G&E-A

scale would be the person who lives in
a freshly built house, has a new car,
wears only new clothes (no thrift-store
shopping), constantly throws slightly
used items away, and eats only half of
his dinner. These people have no eco-
logical awareness. Do they ever think
of a tree, oxygen, or ozone when they're
looking to buy a wooden dining set in
a furniture store? To be good citizens,
these consumers should furnish their
homes from the street. They ought to
gather chairs from the piles of discard-
ed items next to the curbs. They ought
to check for food in the dumpsters

outside Balducci's and Dean & DeLuca.
They ought to be there when friends
spring-clean. And there ought to be a
law against filling up more than one
Hefty garbage bag daily. It ought to be
a punishable crime.

Punishment for this crime would
be a month as a homeless, penniless,
aimless person in a city where the
accused knows no one. In a week this
person will begin to understand the
delicate balance of nature. No longer
will he blindly tip the scales with his
garbage.

The real dilemma in America is that

we don't have more of these valuable
homeless citizens and bag people. We
need them desperately. They ought to
be encouraged. They ought to be pro-
vided with outdoor shelter, like the
Japanese-made lockable cubicles that
were planned to arrive in NYC in the
fall but were vetoed by the city's Human Resources Administration as
"dehumanizing." In Japan these rec-
tangular sleeping quarters serve as
private hotel rooms for $40 a night.
Just think what homeless people could
accomplish with their own little private
shelters. After a night of really decent

sleep they could work doubly hard at the recycling job.

Take a look at India. See any garbage or wasted food lying around the street? Enterprising Indians gather everything edible, saleable, reusable, wearable. Certainly there is a larger population there, fewer jobs, and less shelter. The population outweighs the available housing, so as the only recourse people live on the streets. But they don't really consider themselves homeless. They have little cardboard huts to live in. Life goes on. Families grow, eat, give birth on the street. This is home sweet home.

As the population grows in America and the garbage continues to pile up, we'll have to recruit and pay people to become phony bag people. This is the only solution. Right now these people are working for free. What a bargain! Give them change whenever you pass them. Save up dimes to hand out. Be sure to praise the wonderful bag people, homeless, and beggars. When you hand them the dimes tell them they're doing an excellent job out on the streets. Tell them, "Keep up the good work!" Make them feel as important as they are. These are good people, the righteous few. Shake their hands, smile, give them encouragement at all their corners. They rightfully own the corners. It's their streets, their city, their country, their planet. What have you done today for the planet?

So let us for a moment ease our preconceptions of right and wrong, good and bad. Just as time doesn't exist in universal eternity, neither do good and bad. Suddenly good and bad rush into each other. They don't mean anything, really. But you probably can't bring your self to believe that bag people are better than you are. You probably balk at the very idea that you, a good-looking, smartly dressed, well-fed person, are less important to the world than a dirty bum. Surprise! You are unnecessary! You might as well not have been born. Who needs you, if you continue to make all that garbage? Even artistic contributions to posterity mean nothing compared to the jobs of the street people. These are our truly important folk! Our selfless, beatific, resplendent souls. They ought to be wearing the crowns! We should fall down on our knees in front of them and pay them homage.